A LITT

B O O K

of

Viennese Pastries

JENI WRIGHT

Illustrated by AISLINN ADAMS

CHRONICLE BOOKS

SAN FRANCISCO

First published in 1995 by
The Appletree Press Ltd, 19–21 Alfred Street,
Belfast BT2 8DL
Tel. +44 (0) 1232 243074
Fax +44 (0) 1232 246756
Printed in the E.U. All rights reserved.
Copyright © 1995 The Appletree Press Ltd.

A Little Book of Viennese Pastries

First published in the United States in 1995 by
Chronicle Books, 275 Fifth Street,
San Francisco, CA 94103

ISBN 0-8118-1175-1

9 8 7 6 5 4 3 2 1

For my children, Oliver and Sophie

Introduction

Is it any wonder that from a city as elegant and beautiful as Vienna should come such a wonderful array of cakes and pastries? This city of literally thousands of pastry shops and coffee houses has a long and illustrious tradition of baking. For the Viennese, eating cakes and pastries is one of life's richest – and oldest – pleasures.

It began over five hundred years ago, when Emperor Frederick V of Austria ordered bread rolls to be stamped with his likeness. It seems that from then on, Austrian bakers never looked back. Over the centuries, and particularly in the days when Vienna was the capital of the vast and wealthy Austro-Hungarian Empire, more and more recipes for exquisite cakes, breads, and pastries were created; Viennese bakers fought with each other over whose were the best. Cakes which are now world-famous, such as *Sachertorte* and *Doboztorte*, were invented in Vienna; so too was *Apfelstrudel* and the distinctively shaped *Gugelhupf*, not to mention an incredible number of chocolate gâteaux, nut cakes, and fresh fruit tarts.

The coffee houses of Vienna are still filled today with customers lingering over a coffee and enjoying a pastry – and maybe indulging themselves with an extra helping of *Schlagobers*, the famous whipped cream so beloved by the Viennese. In this charming little cookbook, you will find many of the famous Viennese specialties, plus some lesser-known but no less delicious recipes of the kind made at home. *Guten Appetit!*

A note on measures
Spoon measurements are level unless otherwise indicated.

Vanilla Crescents

Vanillekipferl

These sweet little cookies were traditionally a Christmas specialty, but nowadays they are baked all year round. Take care when baking them that they do not brown – they should be pale in color so that they taste light and buttery. If overbaked, they become brittle and will taste singed.

Pastry:	1 egg yolk
1 ¼ cups all-purpose flour	pinch of salt
½ cup unsalted	2 tsp vanilla sugar (see below)
butter, softened	**To finish:**
3 tbsp confectioners' sugar	⅓ cup confectioners' sugar
½ cup ground almonds	2 tsp vanilla sugar
(makes about 25)	

Preheat oven to 350°F. Put all ingredients in a bowl and knead with your hands to a firm dough. Cover and chill for 1 hour.

Break off walnut-sized pieces of dough and roll each piece into a sausage shape about 2½ inches long. Form into about 25 crescent shapes with tapered ends.

Put the crescents on a greased and floured baking sheet and bake for 20 to 25 minutes. Sift the confectioners' and vanilla sugars onto a plate. Take the crescents from the oven and immediately roll them in the sugar mixture. Place on a rack and sprinkle with the remaining sugar. Leave to cool before serving.

Note: Make vanilla sugar by keeping a vanilla bean pod in a jar of superfine sugar. Use as needed.

The Emperor's Gugelhupf

Kaisergugelhupf

Gugelhupf is said to have been made originally for the Emperor Franz Joseph I. There are many different versions, some made with yeast, some quite plain without the raisins and almonds, and others with a liberal coating of confectioners' sugar. This version is quick and simple because it is made with baking powder. The chocolate icing gives it a luxurious finishing touch.

Pastry:	4 eggs
³/₄ cup raisins	1³/₄ cups all-purpose flour
2–3 tbsp rum	2 tsp baking powder
1 cup unsalted butter, softened	³/₄ cup flaked or chopped
1 cup superfine sugar	almonds
1 tbsp vanilla sugar (see p. 4)	**Icing:**
finely grated zest of 1 lemon	7 oz plain chocolate, chopped
pinch of salt	a knob of butter
(serves 12–14)	

Preheat oven to 350°F. Soak the raisins in the rum for about 10 minutes. In a separate bowl, beat together the butter, sugars, lemon zest, and salt until light and fluffy. Beat in the eggs one at a time, then beat in the flour sifted with the baking powder. Carefully fold in the raisins and rum with the almonds. Pour into a greased and floured 5-cup bundt pan and bake for about 50 minutes or until springy to the touch. Invert onto a rack. To make the icing: Melt the chocolate and butter in a bowl over a pan of hot water, then immediately spread it over the cake while the cake is still warm. Leave to cool before serving.

Austrian Applecake

Österreichischer Apfelkuchen

Although always described as a cake, this is in fact a large sweet tart with a gooey apple filling. Any dessert apples can be used, but Golden Delicious are especially good. Be sure to spread the icing over the top of the cake as soon as the cake comes out of the oven. If the cake is left to go cold before it is iced, the icing will crack.

Pastry:	¹/₂ tsp vanilla sugar (see p. 4)
1¹/₂ cups all-purpose flour	¹/₂ tsp rum
¹/₂ cup superfine sugar	1 cup chopped or flaked
¹/₂ cup unsalted	almonds
butter, cut into pieces	finely grated zest and juice of
1 egg, beaten	1 lemon
¹/₂ tsp ground cinnamon	1 tbsp seedless raspberry jam
Filling:	**Icing:**
1 lb dessert apples	1 cup confectioners' sugar
¹/₂ cup superfine sugar	2 tbsp lemon juice
¹/₂ cup water	¹/₂ egg white
(serves 10–12)	

Preheat oven to 400°F. To make the pastry: Put all ingredients in a bowl and mix with your hands to make a firm dough. Chill for 30 minutes. Peel and core the apples, then dice. Put the superfine sugar in a pan with the water, vanilla sugar, and rum. Bring to a boil, then add the apples, almonds, and lemon zest and juice. Simmer gently, stirring frequently, for about 30 minutes or until the apples are soft and jelly-like. Leave to cool. Roll out the dough on a lightly floured surface and use to line an 11-inch fluted flan mold. Prick dough with a fork, then spread with the jam and spoon in the cold apple filling.

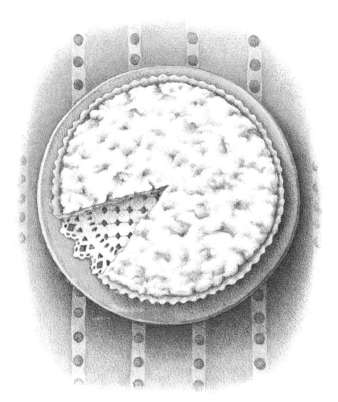

Bake for 30 minutes.

To make the icing: Mix the confectioners' sugar with the lemon juice and egg white, then spread over the top of the warm cake. Leave to cool before serving.

Plum Cake with Cinnamon Streusel

Pflaumenkuchen mit Zimtstreusel

This cake has a yeasted base rather like a sweet pizza dough, and a wonderfully moist plum topping. Arrange the plums on the dough like little canoes with their skins facing downwards. This way, the juice from the plums will not seep into the dough and make it soggy.

---

4 cups all-purpose flour	**Streusel topping:**
pinch of salt	1 1/2 cups all-purpose flour
2 tbsp dried yeast	1/2 cup unsalted butter,
1/3 cup superfine sugar	cut into pieces
1 cup lukewarm milk	1/4 cup superfine sugar
1/2 cup unsalted butter, softened	1 tsp ground cinnamon
2 lb red plums	
(makes about 20 squares)	

Preheat oven to 400°F. Sift the flour and salt into a bowl, make a well in the center and put in the yeast. Add 1 tablespoon of the sugar and 5 tablespoons of the milk to the well and mix with the yeast to make a batter. Leave for 5 minutes.

Gradually cream the butter into the bowl, sprinkle in the remaining sugar, then add the remaining milk and knead with your hands to make a smooth, elastic dough. Leave to rise in a warm place for about 1 hour or until almost doubled in size. Meanwhile, halve and pit the plums, then cut each half in half or quarters, depending on their size. Roll out the dough on a lightly floured surface and use to line a buttered 17-by-14-inch baking tray. Arrange the plum pieces, skin side down, on the dough. Mix together the streusel ingredients and sprinkle over the plums. Bake for 30 to 40 minutes or until the base is golden and the plums cooked through. Serve warm or cold, cut into squares.

Raspberry Cream Roulade

Himbeerroulade

This is a large cake for a special occasion. The cake itself is light and airy, while the typically Austrian filling of farmers' cheese, whipped cream, and fresh raspberries lightly set with gelatin is luxuriously rich. As the *roulade* is rather large you may not have a plate long enough to serve it on, in which case you should cut it into slices to serve, and arrange the slices overlapping in a circular pattern on a large round plate or cake stand.

Pastry:	Filling:
6 eggs, separated	whites of 3 eggs
$^1/_2$ cup superfine sugar	$^1/_2$ cup whipping cream
2 tbsp vanilla sugar	$^1/_4$ cup superfine sugar
pinch of salt	1 tbsp vanilla sugar (see p. 4)
1$^1/_4$ cups all-purpose flour	1 sachet gelatin powder
	1 scant cup farmers' cheese
	2 cups fresh raspberries
	1–2 tbsp confectioners' sugar

(makes 12 slices)

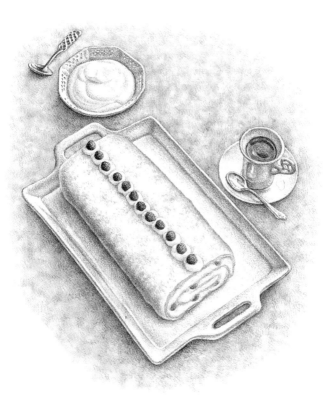

To make the cake: Preheat oven to 425°F. Beat the egg whites with 2 tablespoons of the sugar until stiff. In another bowl, mix the egg yolks with the remaining sugar, vanilla sugar, and salt, until creamy. Fold in the beaten egg whites and then the flour a spoonful at a time. Spread in a greased and parchment-lined 17-by-14-inch baking tray and bake for 10 to 12 minutes, until springy to the touch.

Immediately invert the cake onto a sheet of wax paper sprinkled with superfine sugar. Starting at one end, carefully rub a dampened cloth over the lining paper and peel the paper away from the cake as you rub. While the cake is still warm, carefully roll it up from one of the long ends. Leave to cool, seam side down.

To make the filling: Beat the egg whites until stiff. Whip the cream with the sugars and fold in the beaten egg whites. Dissolve the gelatin in 4 tablespoons water according to packet instructions, then blend into the cheese. Fold the whipped cream into the cheese. Unroll the *roulade*. Reserve a little of the cheese filling for the decoration, then spread the remainder over the *roulade*. Dot with the raspberries, reserving 12 for decoration. Leave the filling for about 10 minutes until just beginning to set, then roll up the *roulade* as before. Sift over the confectioners' sugar, then pipe 12 little rounds of the reserved cheese filling in a line on top and put a raspberry in the center of each one. Keep in a cold place until serving time. Cut into slices with a hot knife.

Little Nut Horns

Nußbeugel

With their gooey, nutty filling, and sweet, rich dough, these little pastries are so unbelievably good that you may very well find they disappear within minutes of being taken out of the oven.

Pastry:	Filling:
1 3/4 cups all-purpose flour	4 oz blanched almonds
1/3 cup unsalted butter, softened	4 oz walnut halves
2 tbsp confectioners' sugar	4 oz shelled and skinned
2 tsp dried yeast	hazelnuts
1 egg yolk	1/2 cup confectioners' sugar
3 tbsp milk	2 tbsp unsalted butter
pinch of salt	1/2 cup milk
1 egg yolk mixed with a little	2 tbsp vanilla sugar (see p. 4)
egg white, to glaze	1 tsp ground cinnamon

(makes 10)

Preheat oven to 375°F. To make the pastry: Put all the ingredients in a bowl and mix with your hands. Gather into a ball and leave aside for about 30 minutes. Meanwhile, grind all the nuts together in a food processor. Bring the remaining filling ingredients to a boil in a heavy pan. Stir in the nuts and boil, stirring constantly, until the mixture becomes a thick and creamy mass. Leave to cool.

Divide the dough into 10 equal pieces. Roll each piece into a sausage shape about 7 inches long and 4 inches wide and make a well in the center. Put 2 heaping tablespoons of filling in the center of each piece of dough, leaving a 1-inch border all around. Fold in the sides over the filling and press to seal, then place the pieces of dough on a greased baking sheet and form into horseshoe shapes with the seams in the center. Fold in the ends of the horseshoes to seal in the filling completely.

Brush the nut horns with the egg glaze and leave aside for about 30 minutes in a cool place. Brush again with egg glaze, then bake for 20 minutes. Serve warm or cold.

Raspberry and Almond Tartlets

Ischler Törtchen

These sweet little tartlets are named after Bad Ischl, where Emperor Franz Josef had his summer residence. Traditionally they are round in shape, but these star shapes look much prettier, and are ideal for a Christmas treat. You can, of course, make them any shape you like.

---

1 1/2 cups all-purpose flour	pinch of salt
1/2 cup ground almonds	2/3 cup unsalted butter, softened
1/2 cup confectioners' sugar	2–3 tbsp raspberry jam
2 tbsp vanilla sugar (see p. 4)	

(makes 20)

Preheat oven to 350°F. Mix all the ingredients, except the jam, and knead until firm. Chill for about 30 minutes. Roll the dough out on a floured surface until about 1/8 inch thick. The dough will be very sticky so make sure that the surface and rolling pin are well floured. Cut out 40 star shapes using a small cookie cutter, then cut out a tiny hole in the center of half the stars. Put all the stars on greased and floured baking sheets and bake for about 8 minutes or until just light golden. Do not let the stars get brown. Sift confectioners' sugar over the stars with the holes in while they are still warm. Leave to cool. Spread jam on the stars without holes, heaping it generously in the center, then press the other stars carefully on top, with the confectioners' sugar facing outwards. The jam will peep through the holes.

Viennese Nut Cake

Wiener Nußkuchen

Recipes for nut cakes can be found all over Austria. This one from Vienna is made with ground hazelnuts. It has fresh bread crumbs in the batter that give the cake a light texture.

Pastry:	3 tbsp apricot jam
1 cup unsalted butter, softened	1 1/2 tbsp water
1 cup superfine sugar	**Icing:**
1 1/2 tbsp vanilla sugar (see p. 4)	1/2 cup superfine sugar
4 eggs	4 oz plain chocolate, chopped
1 3/4 cups all-purpose flour	2 tbsp unsalted butter, softened
1 cup fresh bread crumbs	2 tbsp water
2 tsp baking powder	10–12 whole hazelnuts,
3 tsp cocoa powder	to decorate
1 2/3 cups ground hazelnuts	

(serves 10–12)

Preheat oven to 350°F. Beat the butter, superfine and vanilla sugars, and eggs with an electric mixer until creamy. Add the flour, bread crumbs, baking powder, and cocoa powder and mix until smooth, then add the hazelnuts. Pour the mixture into a greased and floured 5-cup bundt pan and bake for 50 to 60 minutes or until a skewer inserted in the cake comes out clean. Leave to cool in the pan for 10 minutes, then invert onto a plate. Melt the jam with the water in a small pan, work through a sieve, then brush over the cake. Leave to cool.

Mix all the icing ingredients in a pan and heat until smooth. Pour over the cake while still warm and spread with a knife. Decorate with the whole hazelnuts and leave to set before serving.

Christmas Butter Cookies

Weihnachtsgebäck

It is traditional for Austrian families to make special cookies for Christmas, and many families have their own recipe which is passed down from generation to generation. And for those who have no time to make them at home, the bakery shops all over Austria are full of different kinds. This cookie recipe is very quick and easy to do, ideal for those who are in a rush at Christmas but want to carry on an old tradition.

---

²/₃ cup unsalted butter, softened
¹/₂ cup confectioners' sugar
1 egg yolk
2 cups all-purpose flour
2 tbsp vanilla sugar (see p. 4)

1 egg yolk mixed with 1 tbsp water, to glaze
a few tbsp chopped nuts, to garnish

(makes about 40)

Preheat oven to 400°F. Mix the butter, confectioners' sugar, and egg yolk together with your hands. Add the flour and vanilla sugar and knead to a firm dough. Chill for about 2 hours. Roll out the dough on a floured surface until about ¹/₄-inch thick. Cut out about 40 Christmas shapes such as stars, bells, Santa Claus, angels, holly leaves, etc., either freehand or with the appropriate cookie cutters. Place the cookies on baking sheets lined with non-stick baking parchment, brush with the egg glaze and sprinkle with nuts. Bake for 8 to 10 minutes or until lightly colored. Leave to cool on racks before serving.

Marble Cake

Marmorkuchen

This is a plain tea-time cake with a difference – white and chocolate mixtures marbled together. Everyone is always intrigued as to how it's done, and yet it's unbelievably simple – once you know how. Serve it sliced, to reveal the pretty marbled effect.

2¹/₂ cups all-purpose flour	2 tbsp vanilla sugar (see p. 4)
2 tsp baking powder	4 eggs
pinch of salt	¹/₂ cup milk
1 cup unsalted butter, softened	3 tbsp cocoa powder
1 cup superfine sugar	confectioners' sugar, to decorate
(serves 8–10)	

Preheat oven to 400°F. Sift the flour with the baking powder and salt. Beat the butter and sugars with an electric mixer until light and fluffy. Beat the eggs one at a time into the creamed mixture, adding a little of the flour mixture with the last egg if the mixture shows signs of curdling.

Fold in the flour mixture, then stir in 2–4 tablespoons of the milk to make a creamy batter. Put two-thirds of the batter into a greased and floured 5-cup bundt pan.

Stir the cocoa powder into the remaining batter, then add the remaining milk. This batter should be much thinner and runnier than the plain one in the pan. Pour the dark batter into the pan and swirl it carefully into the plain batter with a knife. Bake for 50 to 60 minutes or until a skewer inserted in the cake comes out clean. Leave to cool for about 20 minutes, then invert onto a rack and leave to cool completely. Dust with confectioners' sugar before serving.

Carnival Jam Doughnuts

Faschingskrapfen

These doughnuts date back to the early seventeenth century, when they were first made in Vienna for the Fasching celebrations in January and February leading up to Shrove Tuesday (the last day before Lent). There are hundreds of balls during Fasching, and *Krapfen* are always served at them. Traditionally they have a white band around their middles where the hot oil has not reached during frying. You may be lucky enough to have white bands on yours, but don't worry if you haven't – they taste equally good with or without.

2¹/₂ cups all-purpose flour	1 egg
1 tbsp dried yeast	1 egg yolk
2 tsp superfine sugar	¹/₄ cup unsalted butter,
4 tbsp lukewarm milk	melted and cooled
1 tbsp vanilla sugar (see p. 4)	4 tbsp apricot or raspberry jam
¹/₂ tsp ground cinnamon	vegetable oil for deep-frying
pinch of salt	superfine sugar, to decorate
(makes 12–14)	

Mix two-thirds of the flour with the yeast, 1 teaspoon of the superfine sugar and the milk. Leave to rise for about 20 minutes in a warm place. Add the remaining sugar, vanilla sugar, cinnamon, salt, egg, egg yolk, and butter. Beat together until bubbles form on the surface of the batter, then add the remaining flour and knead with your hands until you have a smooth and elastic dough which is not sticky. Leave to rise in a warm place for another 20 minutes.

Roll out the dough on a floured surface until ¹/₄-inch thick, then cut into 24 to 28 round shapes with the rim of a 2¹/₂-inch glass. Put a little spot of jam in the center of half the rounds, then cover with the remaining rounds and press the edges together to seal. Press the rim of the glass over the doughnuts again and cut off any uneven edges. Deep-fry the doughnuts, in batches, in about $^1/_2$ inch of hot oil for a few minutes, until golden brown on each side. Remove from the oil with a slotted spoon and drain on a rack, then roll in superfine sugar before serving. Serve as fresh as possible.

Almond Kisses

Mandelküsse

These pretty little sweetmeats make good *petits fours* to serve with coffee and liqueurs at the end of a dinner party.

$^2/_3$ cup unsalted butter, softened	2 egg yolks
$^1/_3$ cup superfine sugar, plus 1 tbsp	1 egg white, lightly beaten
2 tbsp vanilla sugar (see p. 4)	$1^1/_3$ cups ground almonds
$1^3/_4$ cups all-purpose flour	2 tbsp seedless raspberry jam
(makes about 40)	

Preheat oven to 350°F. Beat the butter, $^1/_3$ cup superfine sugar, vanilla sugar, and egg yolks with an electric mixer until light and fluffy. Sift in the flour and knead quickly with your hands to a firm dough. Form the dough into about 40 nut-sized balls, roll in the beaten egg white, and then in the almonds. Put them on greased baking sheets and make small indentations in the top of each ball with the handle of a teaspoon. Fill the indentations with jam, then sprinkle the balls with the 1 tbsp superfine sugar. Bake for 15 to 20 minutes. Leave to cool before serving.

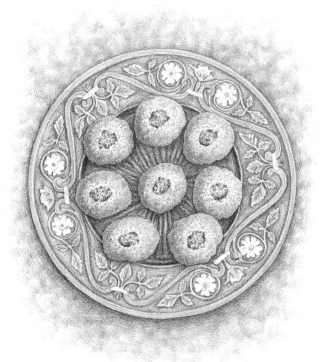

Viennese Fingers

Wiener Plätzchen

These delightful little cookies are perhaps one of the best-known Viennese pastries outside Austria. You can buy them commercially made, but they are very quick and easy to make and the homemade ones taste fresher.

---

1 cup unsalted butter, softened
1/3 cup confectioners' sugar
a few drops of vanilla extract
2 cups self-rising flour
4 oz bittersweet chocolate, chopped
(makes about 20)

Preheat oven to 375°F. Beat the butter, confectioners' sugar, and vanilla extract until pale and creamy. Sift in the flour and beat again until evenly mixed. Pipe the mixture with a star nozzle on to buttered baking sheets, making about 20 three-inch fingers. Space them well apart because they spread during baking. Bake for 10 to 15 minutes, then cool slightly, then transfer to racks and leave until cold. Melt the chocolate in a bowl over a pan of hot water. Remove the bowl from the pan and dip both ends of each finger in the melted chocolate. Return to the racks and leave to set before serving.

Drum Cake

Doboztorte

This classic layer cake can be seen in *pâtisseries* all over Austria. It is quite tricky to make at home, but well worth the effort if you have the time to spare. If you don't have six baking sheets, mark the circles on six sheets of paper as instructed in the recipe, but bake the cake layers in batches according to how many baking sheets you have.

Cake:	**Chocolate cream:**
4 large eggs	1 cup unsalted butter, softened
³/₄ cup superfine sugar	¹/₂ cup confectioners' sugar
1¹/₄ cups all-purpose flour	8 oz plain chocolate, melted
pinch of salt	1 egg yolk
3 oz hazelnuts, toasted and	**Caramel:**
finely chopped, to garnish	²/₃ cup granulated sugar

(serves 12)

Preheat oven to 375°F. Line six baking sheets with non-stick baking parchment and mark an 8-inch circle on each sheet. Put the eggs and sugar in a large bowl over a pan of hot water and beat with a whisk until very thick and pale and the beaters leave a ribbon trail when lifted. Remove the bowl from the pan and continue whisking until the mixture is cold. Sift in the flour and salt and fold in gently with a large metal spoon. Spread the mixture inside the marked circles, then bake for 5 to 6 minutes. As soon as the rounds come out of the oven, transfer them to racks and peel off paper when just cool. To make the chocolate cream: Beat the butter and sugar until pale and creamy, then beat in the melted chocolate and egg yolk. Sandwich five of the six cake layers together with the chocolate

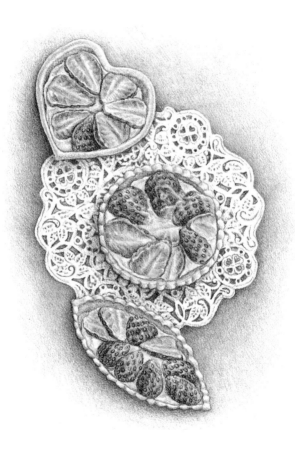

chocolate cream in between and spread it on the top and sides. Press the chopped hazelnuts into the sides.

Put the remaining cake layer on a lightly oiled baking sheet. Melt the granulated sugar in a heavy pan over low heat until it thickens and turns a golden caramel color, then immediately pour over the cake layer. While the caramel is still hot, mark the round into twelve portions with a sharp knife, leave until cold, then place on top of the cake. If there is any chocolate cream left over, it can be used to pipe rosettes around the top edge of the cake.

Little Strawberry Tarts

Erdbeertörtchen

According to the whim of the chef, these little tarts may come in many different shapes.

Pastry:	Filling:
1 cup all-purpose flour	1 cup cream cheese
pinch of salt	juice of 1 lemon
1/4 cup unsalted butter, chilled	5 tbsp red currant jelly
1/2 cup superfine sugar	1 1/3 cups strawberries, hulled
finely grated zest of 1 lemon	and sliced
2 egg yolks	
(makes 12)	

Preheat oven to 375°F. To make the pastry: Sift the flour and salt into a bowl. Add the butter in pieces and work with the fingertips until the mixture resembles bread crumbs. Stir in half the sugar and the lemon zest, then add the egg yolks and mix with the fingertips until the dough draws together. Gather into a ball and chill for 30 minutes.

Roll out the dough on a floured surface and cut out shapes to line 12 individual tartlet molds. Prick the crust and chill for 30 minutes. Line the crust with foil and fill with baking beans. Pre-bake for 15 minutes, remove the foil and beans and bake for a further 3 minutes or until the pastry is crisp and golden. Leave to cool.

To make the filling: Beat the cream cheese with the remaining sugar and half the lemon juice. Remove the pastry shells from the molds. Melt the red currant jelly with the remaining lemon juice and brush inside the pastry shells. Fill with the cream cheese, then arrange the strawberry slices decoratively on top and brush with the remaining red currant jelly. Leave to set before serving.

Apricot and Chocolate Rolls

Rogalach

Originally from a Jewish recipe, these croissant-shaped pastries are absolutely divine, especially when served still warm from the oven.

1 1/4 cups all-purpose flour	5–6 tbsp apricot jam
pinch of salt	2 oz plain chocolate chips
1/2 cup unsalted butter, chilled	melted butter to glaze
scant 1/3 cup farmers' cheese	confectioners' sugar to garnish
(makes 16)	

Preheat oven to 375°F. To make the pastry: Sift the flour and salt into a bowl. Add the butter in pieces and work with the fingertips until the mixture resembles bread crumbs. Stir in the cheese and gather the dough together with the fingertips. Divide the dough

in half, wrap each piece in foil and chill for 1 hour.

Roll 1 piece of dough out on a floured surface to roughly an 8-inch round. Cut the round into 8 triangular wedges. Spread apricot jam on each wedge and then sprinkle with a few chocolate chips. Roll up from the curved edge so that the pointed end is on top. Roll out the remaining piece of dough and repeat. Arrange the rolls on buttered baking sheets and brush with melted butter. Bake for about 15 to 20 minutes or until golden. Sprinkle with confectioners' sugar while still hot.

Sachertorte

This most famous of all Viennese cakes was invented in 1832 by Franz Sacher, chef to Prince Metternich.

Torte:	Glaze:
1/2 cup unsalted butter, softened	4 tbsp apricot jam
1/2 cup confectioners' sugar	2 tbsp water
4 oz plain chocolate, melted	**Icing:**
5 eggs, separated	8 oz plain chocolate, chopped
1/3 cup superfine sugar	1/4 cup vanilla sugar (see p. 4)
3/4 cup all-purpose flour	1 cup confectioners' sugar
	scant 1/2 cup water
(serves 10–12)	

Preheat oven to 350°F. To make the cake: Beat the butter and confectioners' sugar with an electric mixer until light and fluffy. Beat in the melted chocolate and egg yolks. In a separate bowl, whisk the egg whites and superfine sugar until stiff, then fold into the butter and sugar mixture. Sift and fold in the flour in 3 batches.

Pour into a greased and parchment-lined 9-inch springform pan and bake for 1 hour or until a skewer inserted in the center comes out clean. Lift off and discard any crisp crust. Leave the cake to cool in the pan, then turn it out and remove the lining paper.

To make the glaze: Melt the jam with the water in a pan, then work through a sieve and brush over the top and sides of the cake.

To make the icing: Heat three-quarters of the chocolate in a pan with all the other icing ingredients, stirring constantly. Leave to cool slightly, then pour over the top of the cake and spread over the top and sides with a warm butter knife. Leave to set. Melt the remaining chocolate and use a pastry bag to pipe the name "Sacher" on the top of the cake.

Apple Strudel

Apfelstrudel

Viennese *Apfelstrudel* is famous all over the world, but few people realize that the Viennese borrowed the idea for paper-thin leaves of pastry from the Hungarians, who in turn took it from the Turks.

Pastry:	Filling:
12 sheets of frozen filo pastry, thawed	2 lb tart apples
1 cup unsalted butter, melted and cooled	finely grated zest and juice of 1 lemon
³/₄ cup ground almonds	¹/₂ cup raisins
confectioners' sugar, to finish	¹/₃ cup superfine sugar
	¹/₂ tsp ground cinnamon
(serves 8–10)	

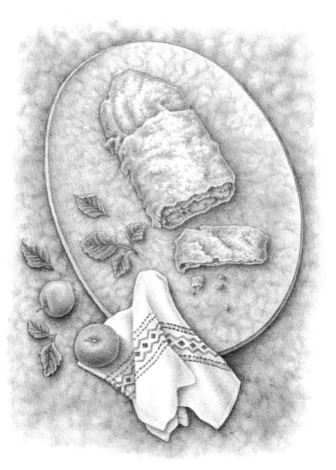

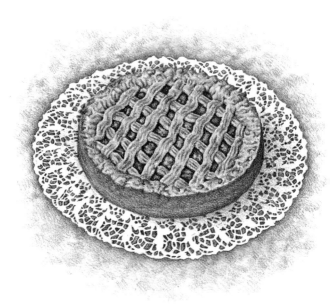

Preheat oven to 400°F. To make the filling: Peel, core, and thinly slice the apples and immediately toss them with the other filling ingredients. Dredge a tea towel with flour and place one sheet of filo on it with the long side facing you. Brush the filo with melted butter. Place another sheet of filo on top of the first and brush with more melted butter. Continue in this way until there are twelve sheets of filo on top of each other with butter in between. Sprinkle the top sheet of buttered filo with the ground almonds, then evenly cover with the filling, leaving a wide border all around the edges. Fold in these edges to seal in the filling, then brush them with melted butter. Using the tea towel to help you, roll up the filo around the filling, starting at the long edge facing you and working away from you. Carefully lift the roll, seam side down, onto a buttered large baking sheet and tuck in the ends so the filling does not ooze out during baking. Brush all over with melted butter and bake for 30 minutes or until crisp and golden. Serve warm, dusted with confectioners' sugar.

Raspberry Tart from Linz

Linzertorte

Pastry:	1 egg, beaten
1 1/2 cups all-purpose flour	4 tbsp red currant jelly, to glaze
pinch of salt	**Filling:**
1/4 cup unsalted butter, chilled	2 1/3 cups raspberries
2/3 cup ground almonds	1 1/4 cups superfine sugar
scant 1/3 cup superfine sugar	2 tbsp arrowroot
(serves 6)	

Preheat oven to 375°F. To make the pastry: Sift the flour and salt into a bowl. Add the butter and work with the fingertips until the mixture resembles bread crumbs, then stir in the almonds and sugar. Add the egg and mix with the fingertips until the dough draws together. Gather into a ball and chill for 30 minutes.

Meanwhile, make the filling: Put the raspberries and sugar in a heavy pan and stir over moderate heat until the sugar has dissolved. Increase the heat and bring to a boil, then simmer, stirring frequently, for 15 to 20 minutes or until the mixture looks like thin jam. In a bowl, mix the arrowroot to a paste with 2 tablespoons water and then stir into the raspberry mixture. Stir until the mixture thickens, then remove from the heat and leave to cool.

Set aside a small ball of dough to make the lattice, then roll out the remaining dough and use to line the bottom and sides of an 8-inch flan mold. Chill for 15 minutes.

Spread the cool filling in the tart shell, then roll out the reserved dough and cut out 8 thin strips. Place the strips over the filling in a lattice pattern, sealing the ends to the crust with a little water. Bake for 35 minutes. Leave the tart to cool in the pan, then warm the red currant jelly until melted and brush all over the top. Leave to set before serving.

Chocolate and Hazelnut Tart

Schokoladen-Haselnuß Torte

Chocolate and hazelnuts are two favorite ingredients of the Viennese. Here they are combined together to make a rich, moist tart. Serve it with *Schlagobers* (whipped cream) for the most luscious of desserts.

Pastry:	$^2/_3$ cup superfine sugar
1$^3/_4$ cups all-purpose flour	2 eggs, beaten
pinch of salt	1 tbsp all-purpose flour
$^2/_3$ cup unsalted butter, chilled	2 cups ground hazelnuts
scant $^1/_3$ cup superfine sugar	3 oz plain chocolate, grated
1 egg, beaten	2 tbsp brandy or rum
Filling:	grated chocolate, to decorate
$^1/_3$ cup unsalted butter, softened	

(serves 8–10)

To make the pastry: Sift the flour and salt into a bowl. Add the butter and work with the fingertips until the mixture resembles bread crumbs, then stir in the sugar. Add the egg and mix with the fingertips until the dough draws together. Gather into a ball, then roll out on a floured surface and use to line a 10-inch tart mold. Prick the bottom and chill for 30 minutes.

Preheat oven to 400°F. To make the filling: Beat the butter and sugar until light and fluffy, then beat in the eggs and flour followed by the hazelnuts, chocolate, and brandy or rum. Put the filling in the tart shell and bake for 25 to 30 minutes or until the filling is set. Leave to cool in the pan. Serve lukewarm, sprinkled with grated chocolate.

Chocolate Truffle Cake

Trüffeltorte

Every *pâtisserie* has its own recipe for chocolate truffle cake, some exceptionally rich and ornate, others more modest. It's all a question of personal taste as to which you like best. This one is smooth and dark, with a very rich *ganache* filling in the center. It is best to cut it into thin slices when serving.

Cake:	Ganache:
2/3 cup unsalted butter, softened	12 oz bittersweet chocolate, chopped
1/2 cup confectioners' sugar	
5 oz bittersweet chocolate, melted	1 1/2 cups heavy cream
	2 tbsp brandy
6 eggs, separated	**Icing:**
1/2 cup superfine sugar	1 cup superfine sugar
1 cup all-purpose flour	1 scant cup water
	7 oz bittersweet chocolate, chopped
	candied rose petals, to decorate

(serves 15)

Preheat oven to 350°F. To make the cake: Beat the butter and confectioners' sugar with an electric mixer until light and fluffy. Beat in the melted chocolate and egg yolks. In a separate bowl, whisk the egg whites and superfine sugar until stiff, then fold into the butter and sugar mixture. Sift and fold in the flour in three stages. Pour into a greased and parchment-lined 9-inch springform pan and bake for 1 hour or until a skewer inserted in the center comes out clean. Leave the cake to cool in the pan, then turn it out and remove the lining paper. Cut the cake horizontally in half and return one half to the pan.

To make the *ganache*: Put the chopped chocolate in a bowl. Heat the cream until very hot, then pour over the chocolate and stir until the chocolate has melted and the mixture is smooth. Stir in the brandy and leave to cool, then beat with the electric mixer until fluffy. Spread the *ganache* on top of the cake layer in the pan, then put the second cake layer on top. Chill for 1 hour.

To make the icing: Put the sugar and water in a heavy pan, heat gently until the sugar has dissolved, then boil without stirring until a white syrup is formed (do not allow it to darken). Add the chocolate and continue boiling until the icing is thick, then pour over the top of the cake and spread evenly over the top and sides. Chill for at least 4 hours before serving decorated with candied rose petals.

Chocolate Truffles

Schokoladentrüffel

If you have any leftover fruit cake, these truffles are an ideal way to use it up.

---

4 oz rich fruit cake, crumbled	4 oz plain chocolate, melted
1 1/4 cups ground almonds	2 tbsp rum
1/3 cup confectioners' sugar	cocoa powder, for coating
(makes about 25)	

Mix the cake crumbs, ground almonds, and sugar, and stir well to blend, then mix in the chocolate and rum. Knead until the mixture comes together, then shape into about 25 balls and roll in cocoa powder. Chill before serving.

Bishop's Bread

Bischofsbrot

This Christmas specialty is traditionally baked in a *Rehrücken* mold, which gives it its characteristic barrel shape. Any small loaf pan may be used.

---

5 eggs, separated
$^1/_2$ cup superfine sugar
3 tbsp unsalted butter, softened
1 cup all-purpose flour, sifted
$^1/_2$ cup flaked almonds
$^1/_3$ cup sultanas or raisins
$^1/_2$ cup dried apricots, finely chopped
$^1/_2$ cup candied mixed peel, finely chopped
(serves about 8)

Preheat oven to 350°F. Beat the egg yolks, sugar, and butter with an electric mixer until creamy. Beat in the flour, then the nuts and fruits.

Whisk the egg whites until stiff, then fold into the batter until evenly incorporated. Pour into a greased and floured 4$^1/_2$-cup *Rehrücken* mold or loaf pan and bake for 40 to 45 minutes or until a skewer inserted in the center comes out clean. Invert onto a rack and leave to cool before serving.

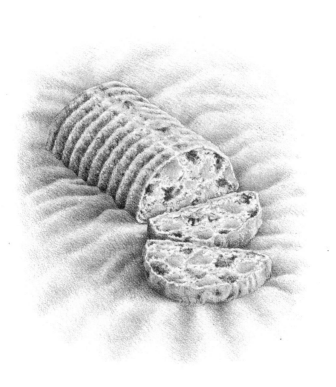

Cherry Cream Slices

Kirschcremeschnitten

Layers of crisp, light puff pastry, rich *crème pâtissière*, sweet ripe cherries, and kirsch make luscious melt-in-the-mouth pastries.

2 egg yolks	8 oz frozen puff pastry,
1/4 cup superfine sugar	thawed
1/2 cup cornstarch	1 1/4 cups heavy cream
1 1/4 cups milk	2 2/3 cups cherries
2 tbsp kirsch	
(serves 6)	

Preheat oven to 425°F. Mix the egg yolks, sugar, and cornstarch in a bowl. Scald the milk in a pan, then stir into the egg yolk mixture. Return to the pan and simmer, stirring, until thick. Remove from the heat and stir in the kirsch. Cover the surface of the custard with plastic wrap and leave to cool.

Roll out the pastry on a floured surface to a 14-by-12-inch rectangle. Place on a wetted baking sheet, prick all over with a fork and bake for 10 minutes. Carefully ease the pastry off the sheet, turn it over and return to the oven for 5 minutes or until golden and crisp. Transfer to a rack and leave to cool.

Whip the cream until thick and fold half into the custard. Reserve six whole cherries for decoration, and pit and finely chop the rest. Fold the chopped cherries into the custard cream.

Cut the pastry lengthwise into thirds, place one piece on a serving plate and spread it with the cherry cream. Top with another piece of pastry, the remaining cherry cream and the remaining pastry. Pipe or spread the remaining whipped cream on top and decorate with the whole cherries. Cut into 6 slices to serve.

Saddle of Venison Cake

Rehrücken

So called because it is traditionally baked in a special *Rehrücken* mold to look like a saddle of venison, this cake is rich with chocolate and nuts. The spiky almond decoration is meant to resemble the strips of pork fat used to lard the meat for roasting.

$^1\!/_2$ cup unsalted butter, softened
$^3\!/_4$ cup confectioners' sugar
5 eggs, separated
$^1\!/_2$ cup ground almonds
1 cup fresh bread crumbs
2 oz plain chocolate, melted
1 tsp ground cinnamon
3 tbsp apricot jam
chocolate icing (see Viennese Nut Cake, p. 20)
about 8 whole blanched almonds, cut into sticks, to decorate
(serves about 8)

Preheat oven to 350°F. Beat the butter and sugar with an electric mixer until light and fluffy. Beat in the egg yolks, almonds, bread crumbs, melted chocolate, and cinnamon. Whisk the egg whites until stiff, then fold into the batter until evenly incorporated. Pour into a greased and floured $4^1\!/_2$-cup *Rehrücken* mold or loaf pan and bake for 45 minutes or until a skewer inserted in the center comes out clean. Invert onto a rack and leave to cool.

Melt the jam with $1^1\!/_2$ tablespoons water, then work through a sieve and brush all over the cake. Pour the icing over the cake and press in the almond sticks. Leave to set before serving.

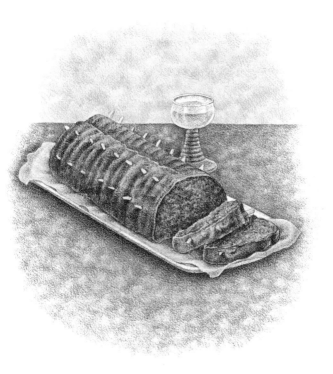

Cheesecake

Topfenkuchen

There are countless versions of *Topfenkuchen* to be found all over Austria, and *Topfen*, the Austrian equivalent of our cottage cheese, is widely used in Austrian baking. This traditional baked cheesecake is rich and sweet, and is especially good for morning coffee, served with *Schlagobers* (whipped cream).

Pastry:	Filling:
1 1/2 cups all-purpose flour	2 cups cottage cheese
pinch of salt	1/4 cup superfine sugar
1/3 cup unsalted butter, chilled	2 eggs, beaten
2 tbsp superfine sugar	3/4 cup raisins
finely grated zest of 1 lemon	finely grated zest and juice of
1 egg, separated	1 lemon

(serves 8)

Preheat oven to 350°F. To make the pastry: Sift the flour and salt into a bowl and work in the butter until the mixture resembles bread crumbs. Stir in the sugar and lemon zest, then the egg yolk and enough water to bind the dough together. Form into a ball, then roll out on a floured surface and use to line a 7-inch springform pan. Brush dough with egg white and chill for 30 minutes.

Put all the filling ingredients in a bowl and beat well to mix. Pour into the pastry-lined pan and bake on a preheated baking sheet for 50 minutes or until the filling is set. Leave to cool in the pan before serving.

Index